Camels

Victoria Blakemore

vblakemore.author@gmail.com

Copyright info/picture credits

Cover, Fotoimp/AdobeStock; Page 3, Dmitry Pichugin/ AdobeStock; Page 5, Wolfgang Zwanzger AdobeStock; Page 7, pixel-mixer/Pixabay; Page 9, Mieszko9/AdobeStock; Pages 10-11, TuendeBede/Pixabay; Page 13, BlueSnap/Pixabay; Page 15, robnaw/AdobeStock; Page 17, Fotoimp/ AdobeStock; Page 19, Oleg Zhukov/AdobeStock; Page 21, NoraDoa/AdobeStock; Page 23; belizar/AdobeStock; Page 25, 2017_Franziska/Pixabay; Page 27, jahmaica/AdobeStock; Page 29, Cheryl/AdobeStock; Page 31, Aleš Nowák/ AdobeStock; Page 33, georgeoprea9/AdobeStock

Table of Contents

What are Camels?   2

Kinds of Camels   4

Physical Characteristics   6

Habitat   8

Range   10

Diet   12

Storing Energy   14

Communication   16

Movement   18

Herd Life   20

Camel Calves   22

Self Defense   24

Lifespan   26

Population   28

Helping People   30

Glossary   34

What Are Camels?

Camels are tall mammals that are known for their large, fatty humps.

Their humps are used to store fat for when food or water are not available.

Camel humps stand up straight when they are healthy and have enough food.

3

Kinds of Camels

There are two different kinds of camels: the **dromedary** camel and the **bactrian** camel.

Bactrian camels have two humps. They usually have longer, thicker patches of hair.

The dromedary camel has

one hump. It is the most

common kind of camel.

Physical Characteristics

Camels have a thick coat of hair that can be many shades of brown.

Their thick coat protects them from the sun. It can also keep them warm at night.

Camels have long eyelashes

that help to keep their eyes

free from sand when it gets

windy.

Habitat

Camels are found in deserts, where it is dry with little plant life.

Bactrian camels are found in the deserts of colder areas. They shed their thick coat of hair in the summer.

Range

Camels can be found in Africa, Asia, and Australia. There are not many left in the wild.

Most are **domesticated**, which means that they live with people.

II

Diet

Camels are **herbivores**, which means that they eat plants. They use their strong lips to tear off parts of plants.

Camels are known to **graze** like cows or sheep. They spend much of their day eating.

Camels have thick skin on their
tongue and in their mouth. It
lets them eat cactus plants
without getting hurt.

Storing Energy

Camels use the fat stored in their humps for energy if food is not available.

They can live for a week without water and for several months without food.

Communication

Camels use sound and movement to communicate with each other.

When a camel wants to give a friendly greeting to another camel, it may blow air in the other camel's face.

Camels can groan, grunt,

bellow, roar, and bleat.

Movement

Camels have large, wide feet. This allows them to walk through the desert sands without sinking in.

They can walk about 20 miles each day and run at speeds of up to 40 miles per hour.

Camels move in an odd way. They move both legs from one side of their body at the same time.

19

Herd Life

In the wild, camels live in

groups that are called herds.

There may be as many as 30

camels in a single herd.

Herds travel together to look

for food and water.

Camels are very **tolerant** of each other, they rarely fight or get **aggressive**.

Camel Calves

Camels usually have one

baby, but can have twins.

Camel babies are called

calves or cria.

Calves are born with weak

legs, so they are wobbly

when they first try to stand

up.

Camel mothers leave the herd when the calf is born. After about two weeks, the mother and calf will join the herd again.

Self Defense

Camels are known to spit if they feel threatened or bothered.

They bring up digested food from their stomach and spit it at whatever is bothering them.

You can tell if a camel is about

to spit by the way they puff up

their cheeks and purse their lips.

Life Span

Camels usually live between 45 and 50 years. In the wild, their life span may be much shorter.

Wild camels are hunted because they may **compete** with domesticated camels for food.

Camels are not fully grown until

they are about seven years old.

Population

Australia is home to the largest number of wild Dromedary camels.

There are estimated to be over one million in the Australian deserts.

There are less than 1,000 wild Bactrian camels in Asia, making them an **endangered** species.

Helping People

Camels have been helping people for hundreds of years. They are used as transportation in the desert, which is why they are sometimes called the "ships of the desert."

When a group of camels are transporting people, they are called a **caravan** of camels.

Camels are able to carry about 200 pounds, so they are used to **transport** people as well as carry supplies.

Camels are also used for milk, meat, wool, and leather.

Glossary

Aggressive: mean, likely to attack

Bactrian: a species of camel that has two humps

Caravan: a group of camels that are transporting people

Compete: try to get something that others are trying to get too

Domesticated: an animal that is tame and kept as a pet or on a farm

Dromedary: a species of camel that only has one hump

Endangered: at risk of becoming extinct

Graze: to feed on grass

Herbivore: an animal that eats only plants

Tolerant: accepting of others

Transport: to carry from one place to another

About the Author

Victoria Blakemore is a first grade

teacher in Southwest Florida with a

passion for reading.

You can visit her at

www.elementaryexplorers.com

Also in This Series

Gray Wolves	Sloths	Flamingos	Camels	Koalas	Honey Bees	Pandas
Pangolins	White-Tailed Deer	Orcas	Giraffes	Corn	Meerkats	Echidnas
Walruses	Raccoons	Bald Eagles	Apples	Arctic Foxes	Red Pandas	Cassowaries
Tigers	Ladybugs	Moose	Beluga Whales	Leopards	Elephants	Jellyfish
Binturongs	Lions	Dolphins	Reindeer	Hammerhead Sharks	Hippos	Pumpkins
Peafowl	Chameleons	Florida Panthers	Aye-Ayes	Black Bears	Cheetahs	Manatees
Gingerbread	Polar Bears	Hot Chocolate	Orangutans	Coyotes	Marshmallows	Strawberries

All titles in the series feature: Elementary Explorers, Victoria Blakemore

Also in This Series

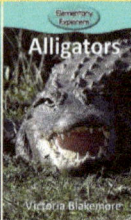

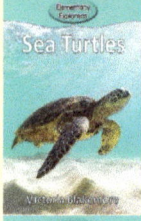

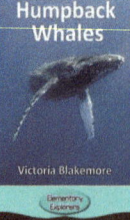

Aardvarks	Mako Sharks	Alligators	Frogs	Hedgehogs	Brown Bears	Bongos
Sea Turtles	Quokkas	Muskrats	Zebras	Red Foxes	Ring-Tailed Lemurs	Platypuses
Anteaters	Kangaroos	Rhinos	Jaguars	Wombats	Capybaras	Gorillas
Cats	Skunks	Butterflies	Dingoes	Snow Leopards	African Wild Dogs	Penguins
Whale Sharks	Wolverines	Warthogs	Caracals	Badgers	Seals	Hummingbirds
Pikas	Humpback Whales	Pumas	Lemonade	Llamas	Tulips	Ostriches
Sunflowers	Fennec Foxes	Sea Lions	Squirrels	Roses	Porcupines	Ice Cream

www.ingramcontent.com/pod-product-compliance
Lightning Source LLC
Chambersburg PA
CBHW042249040426
42336CB00043B/3387